This Book Belong To

COLOR TEST

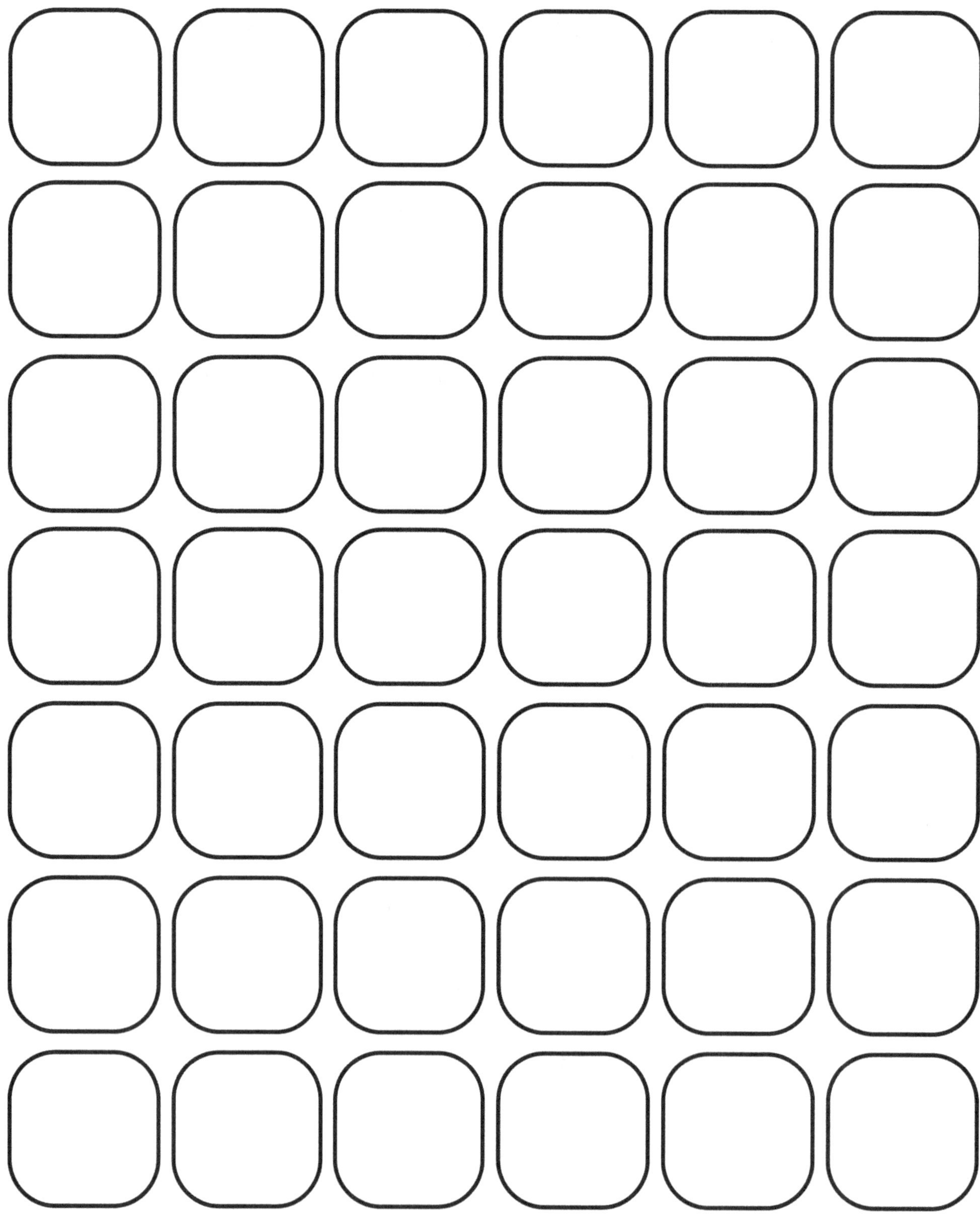

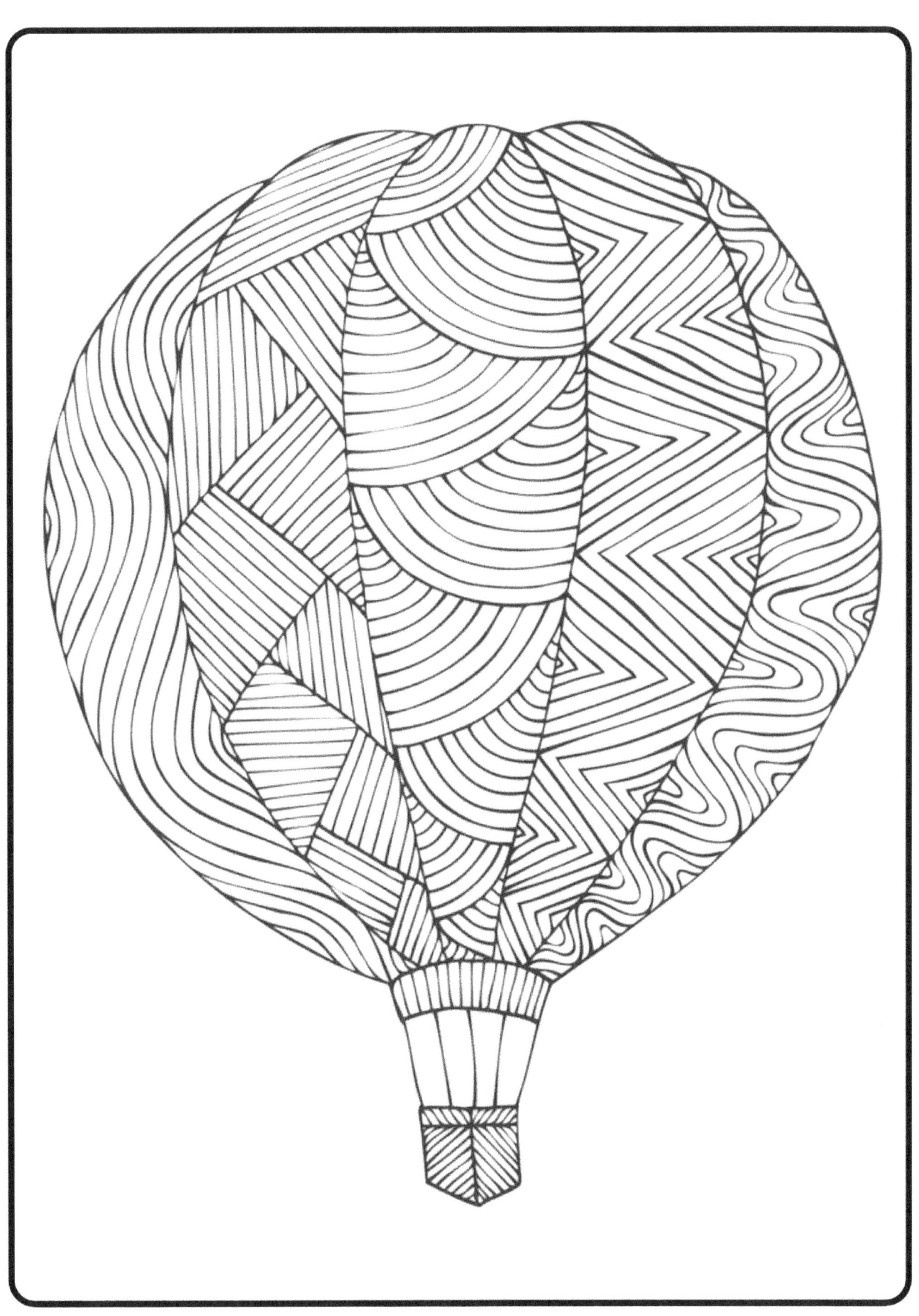

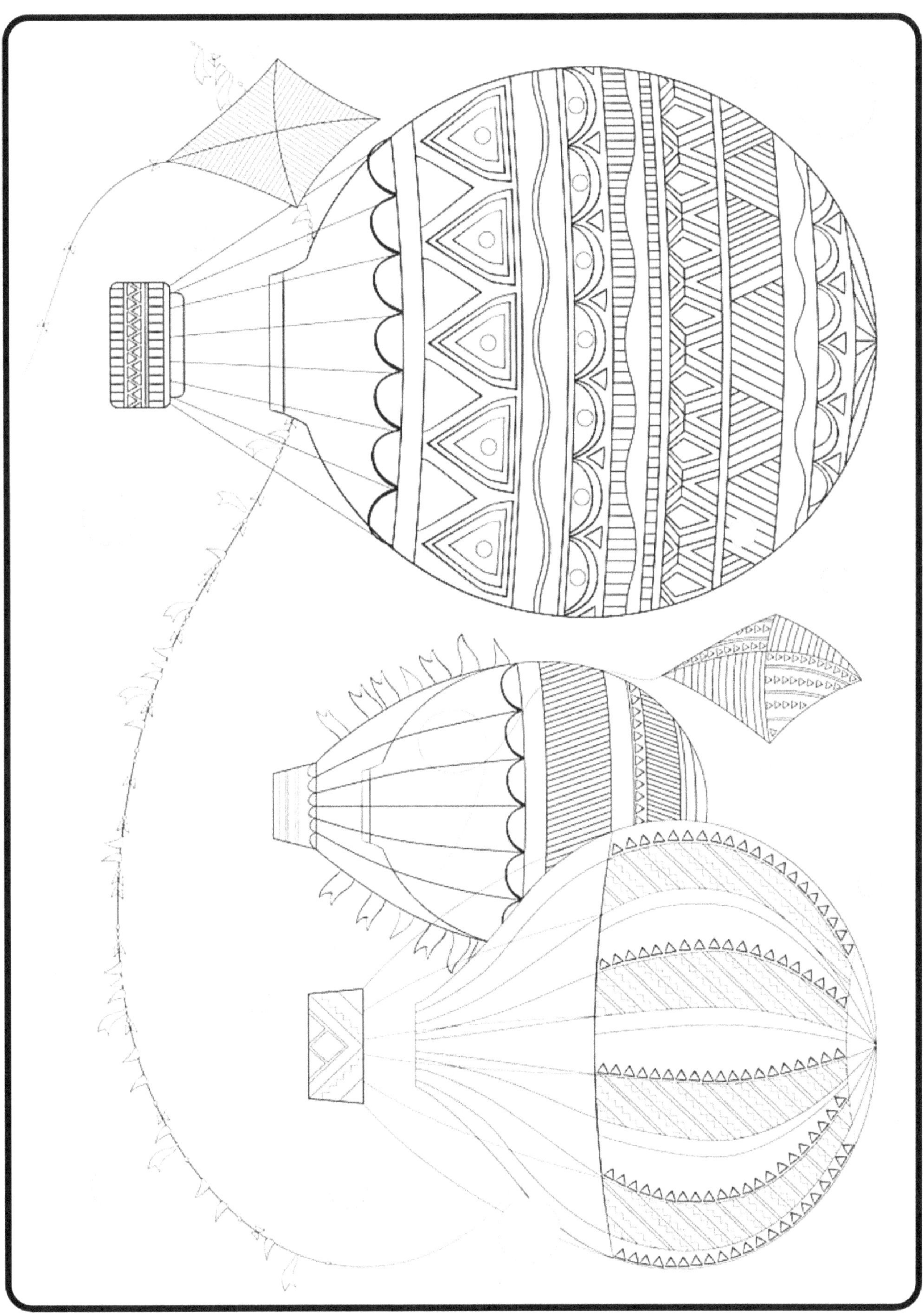

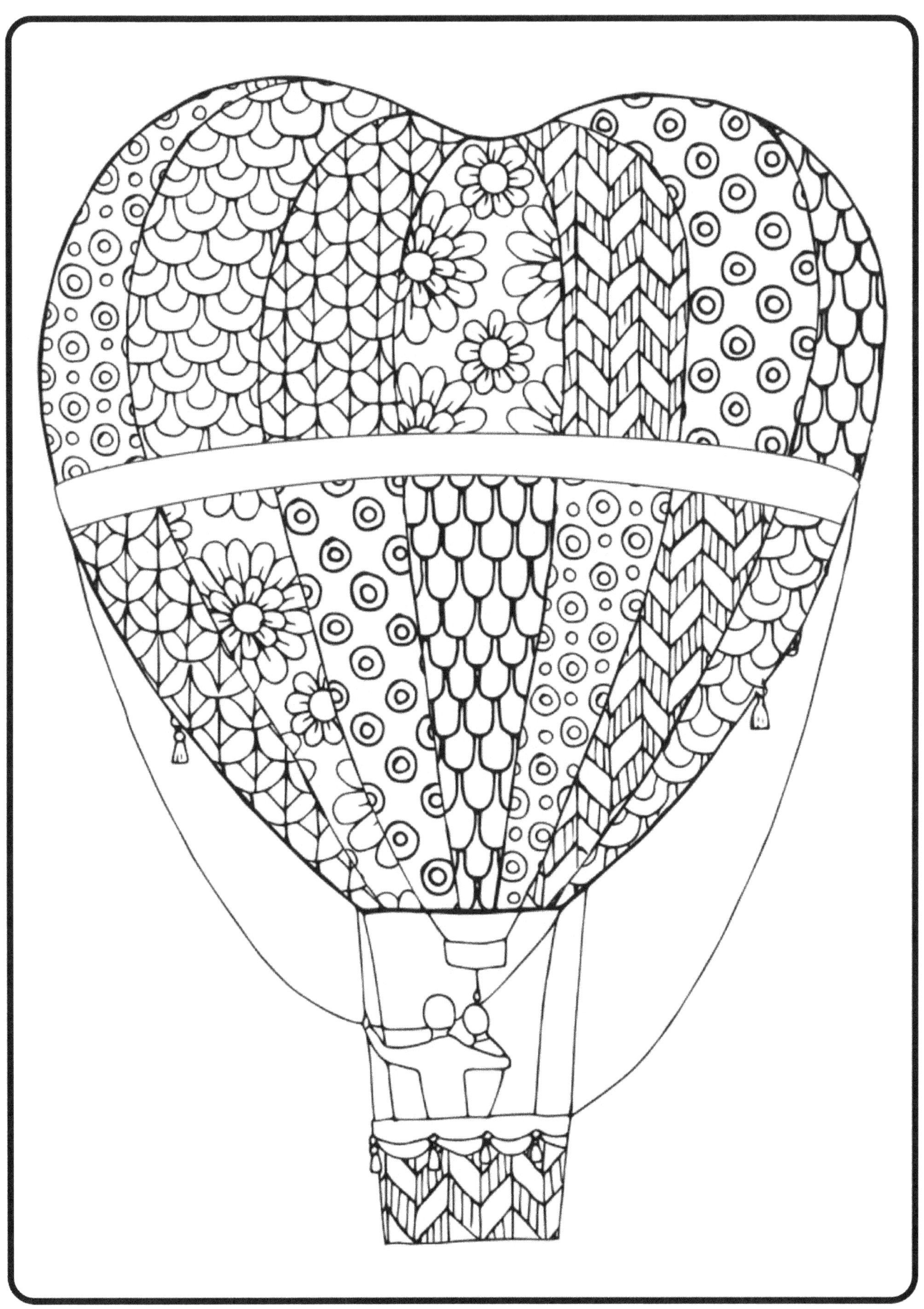

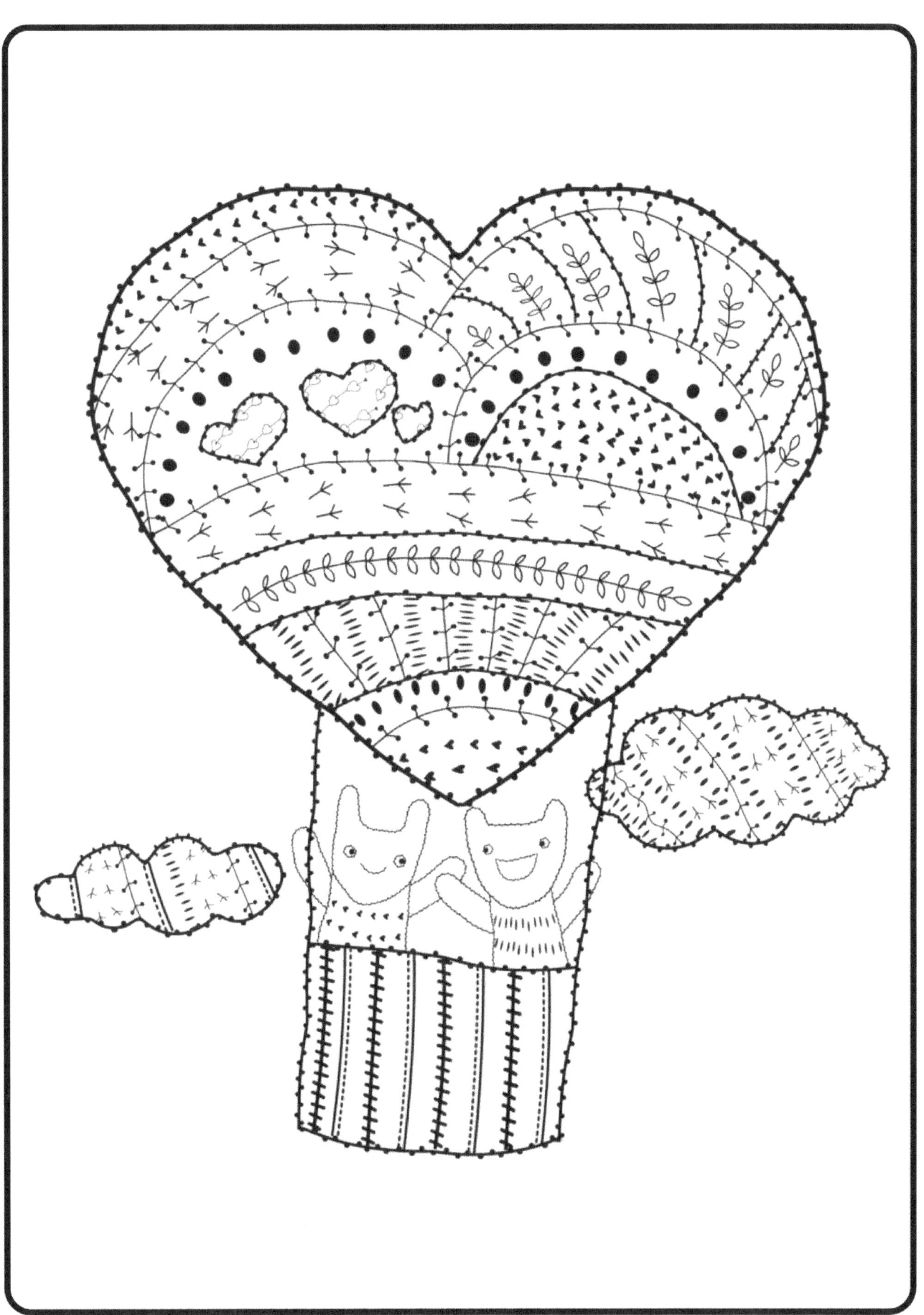

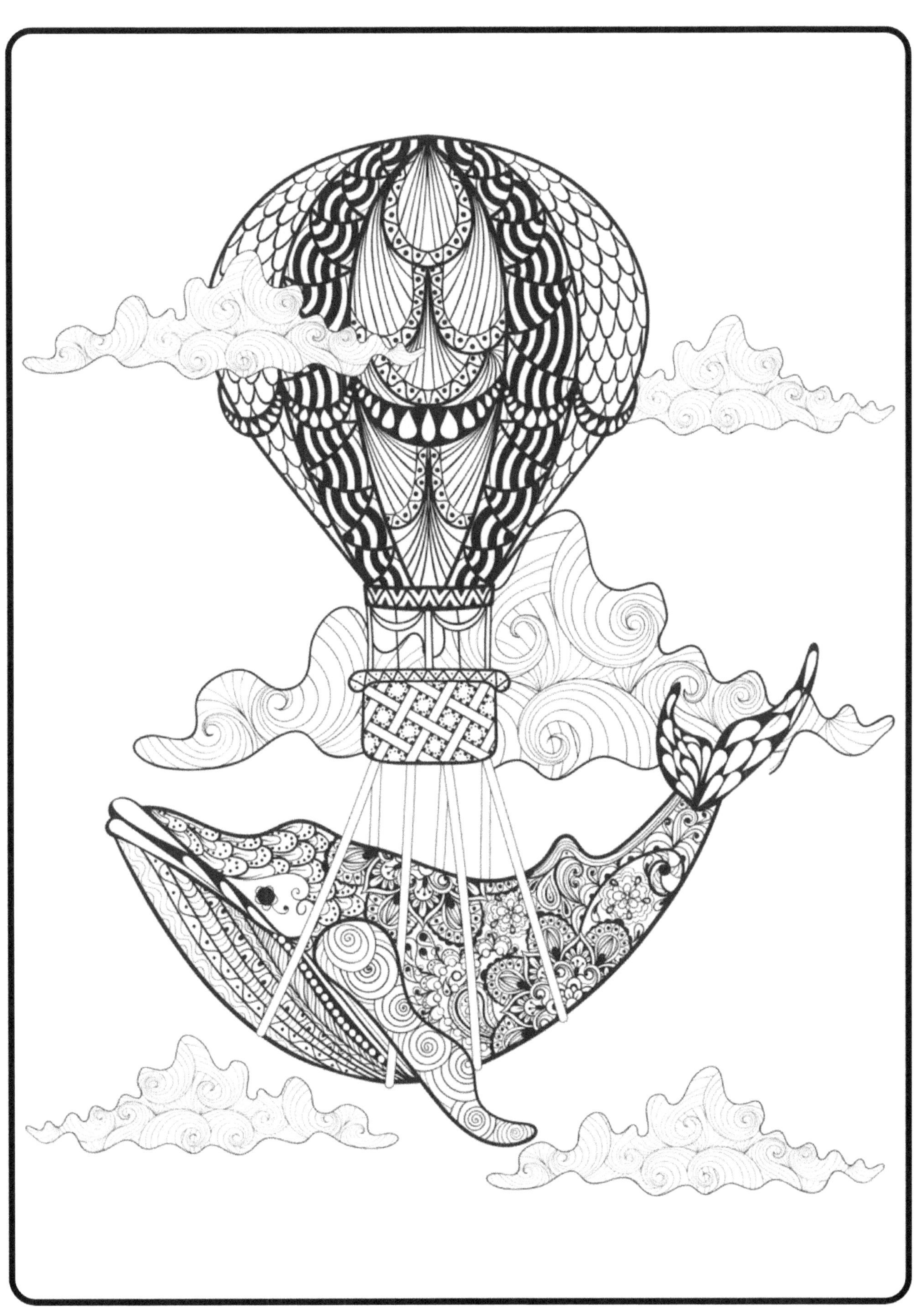

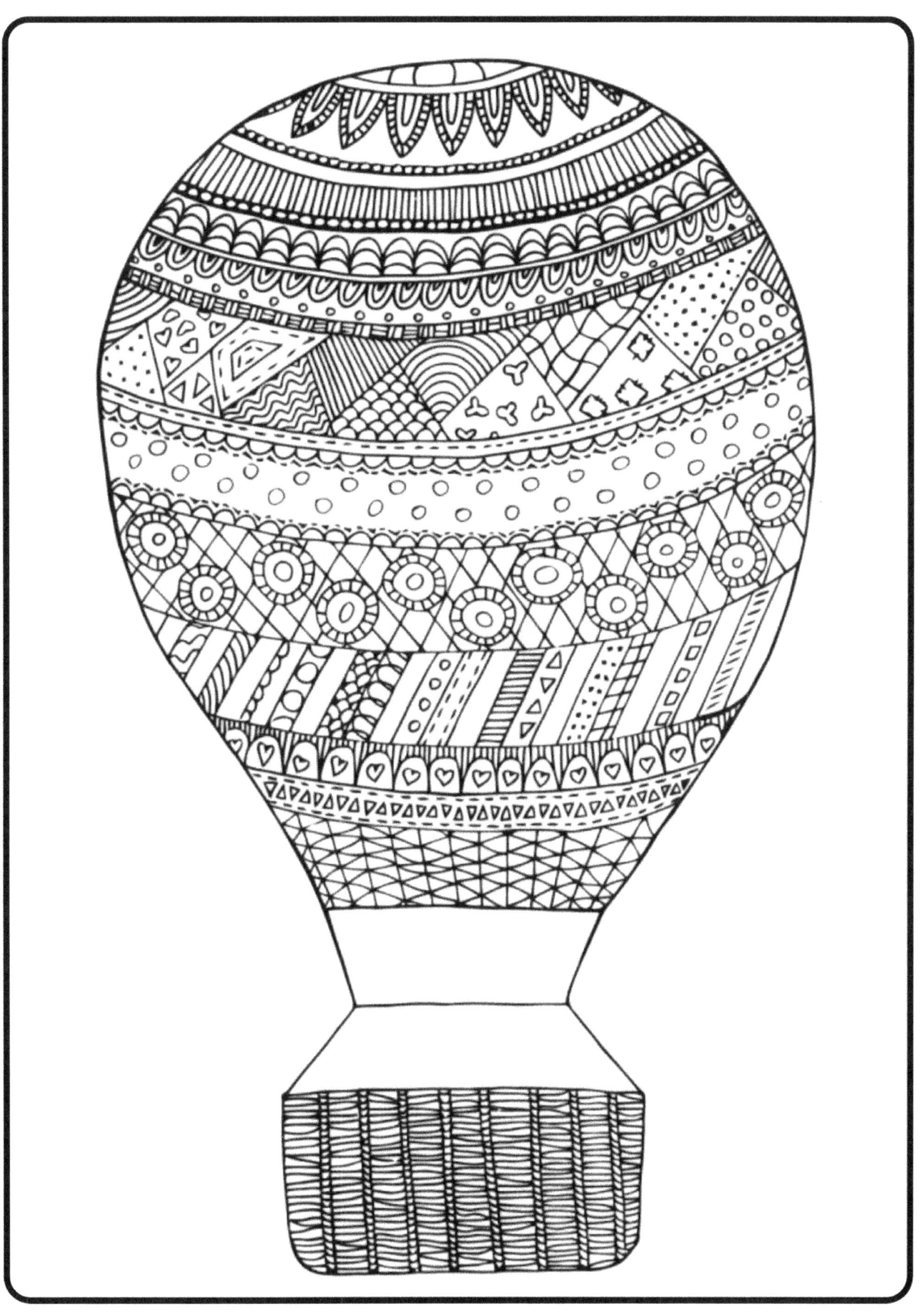

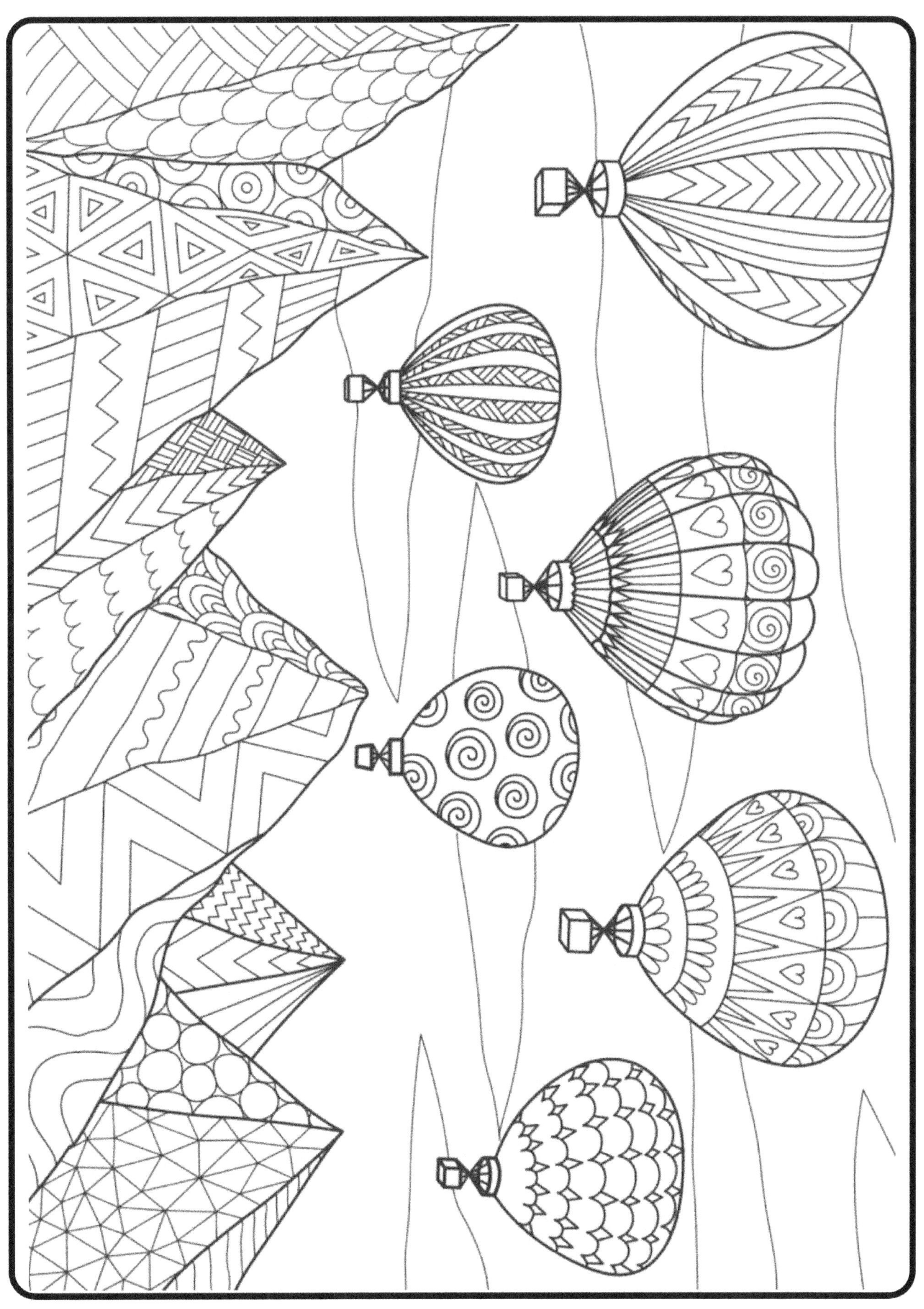

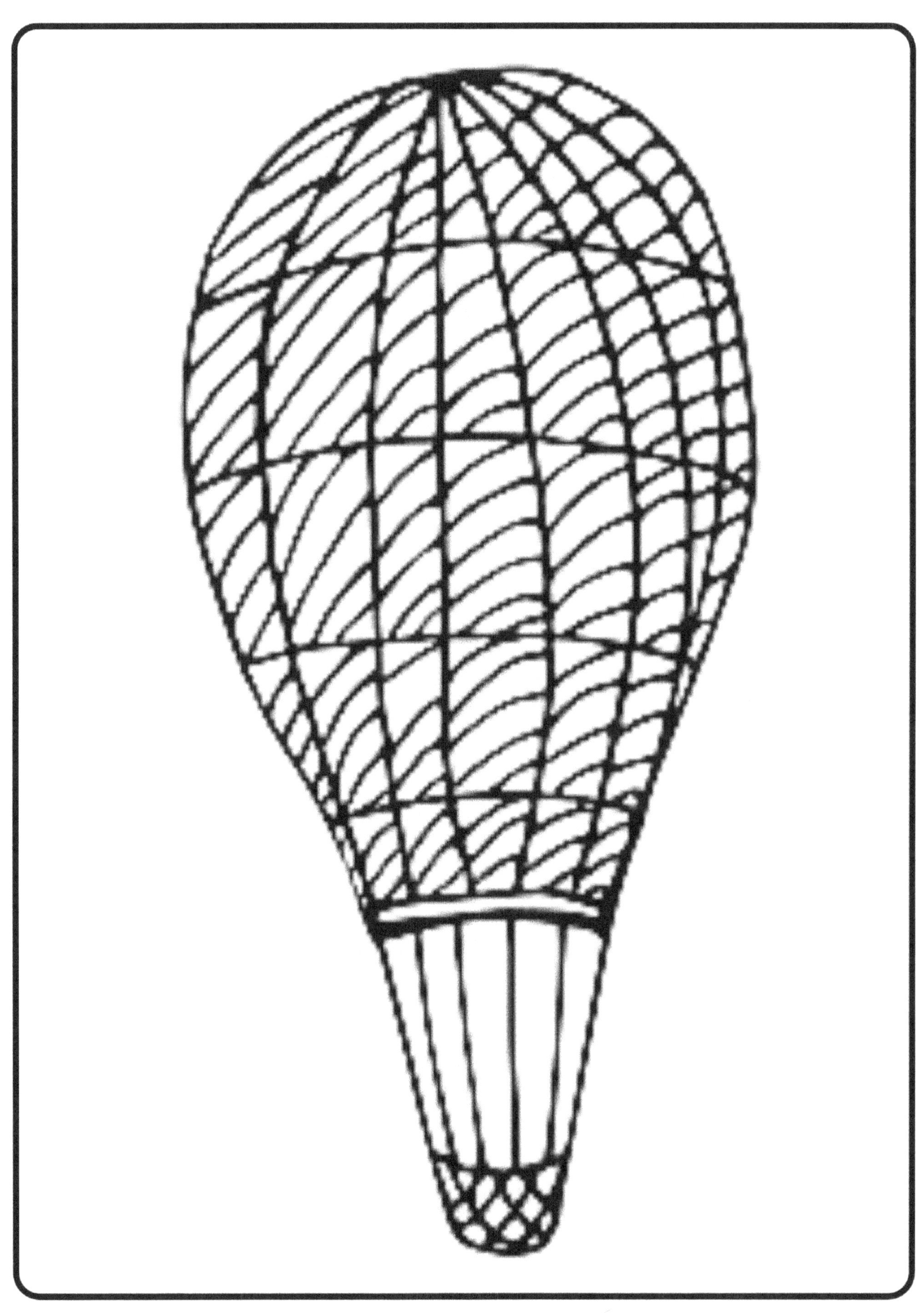

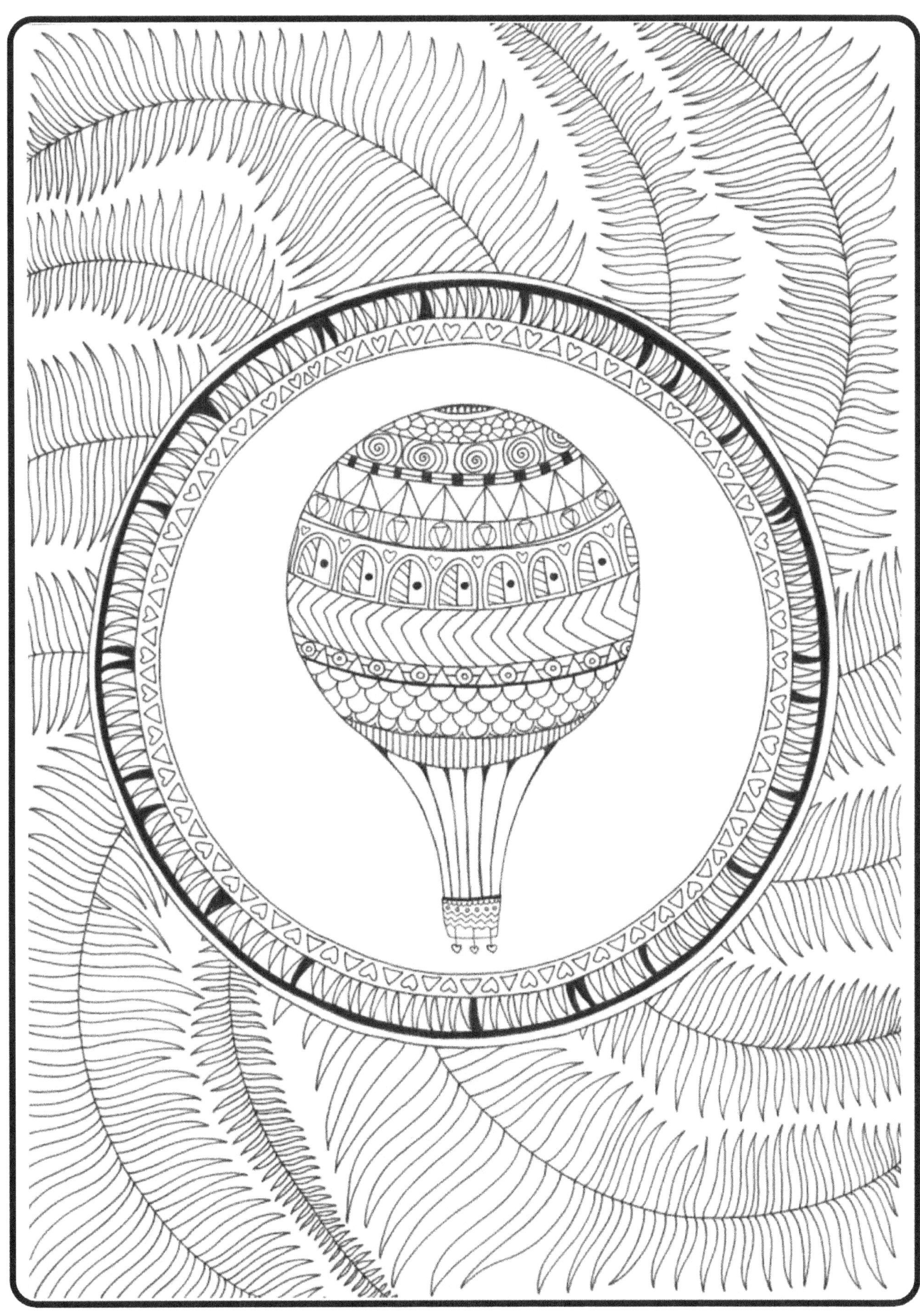

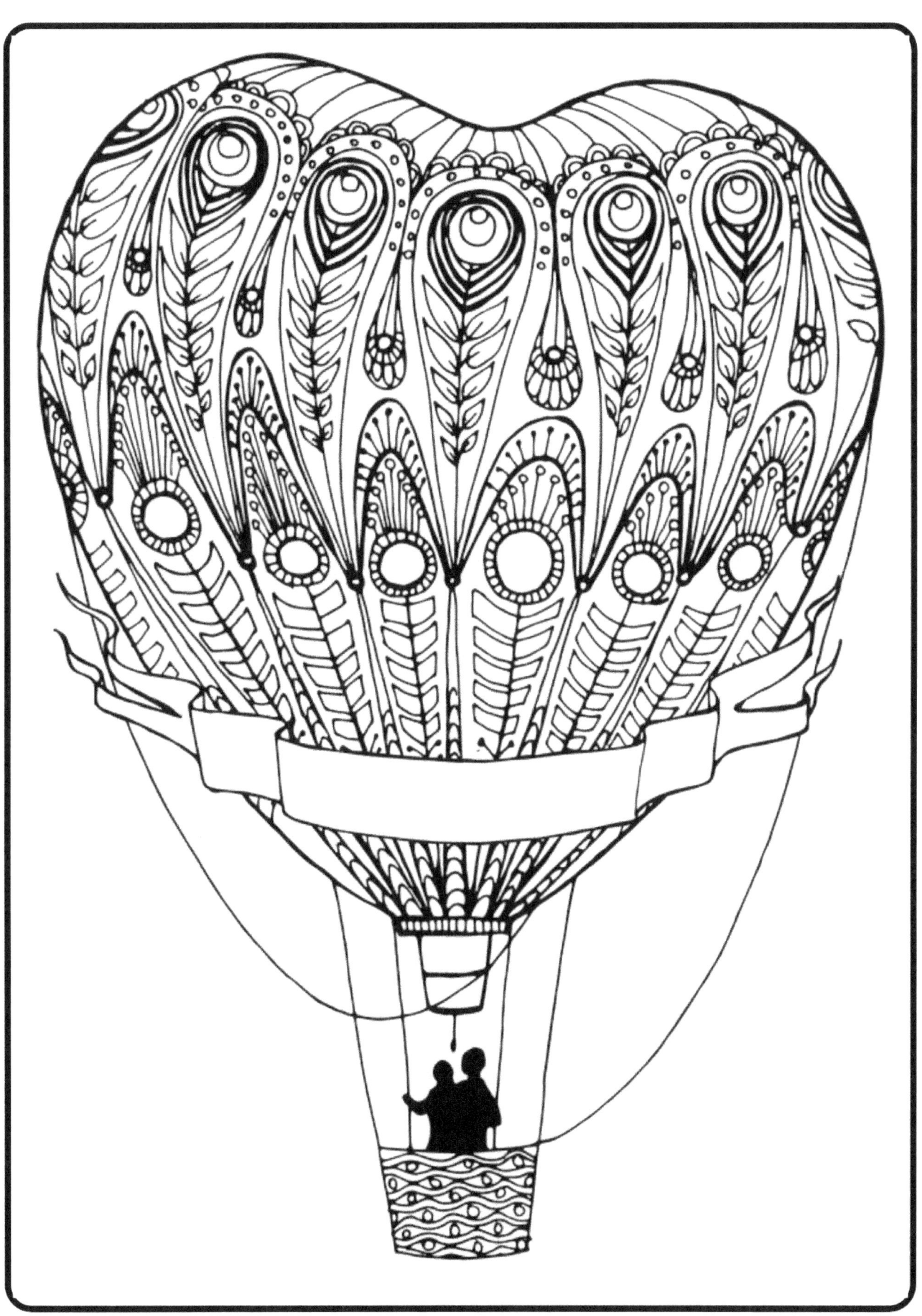

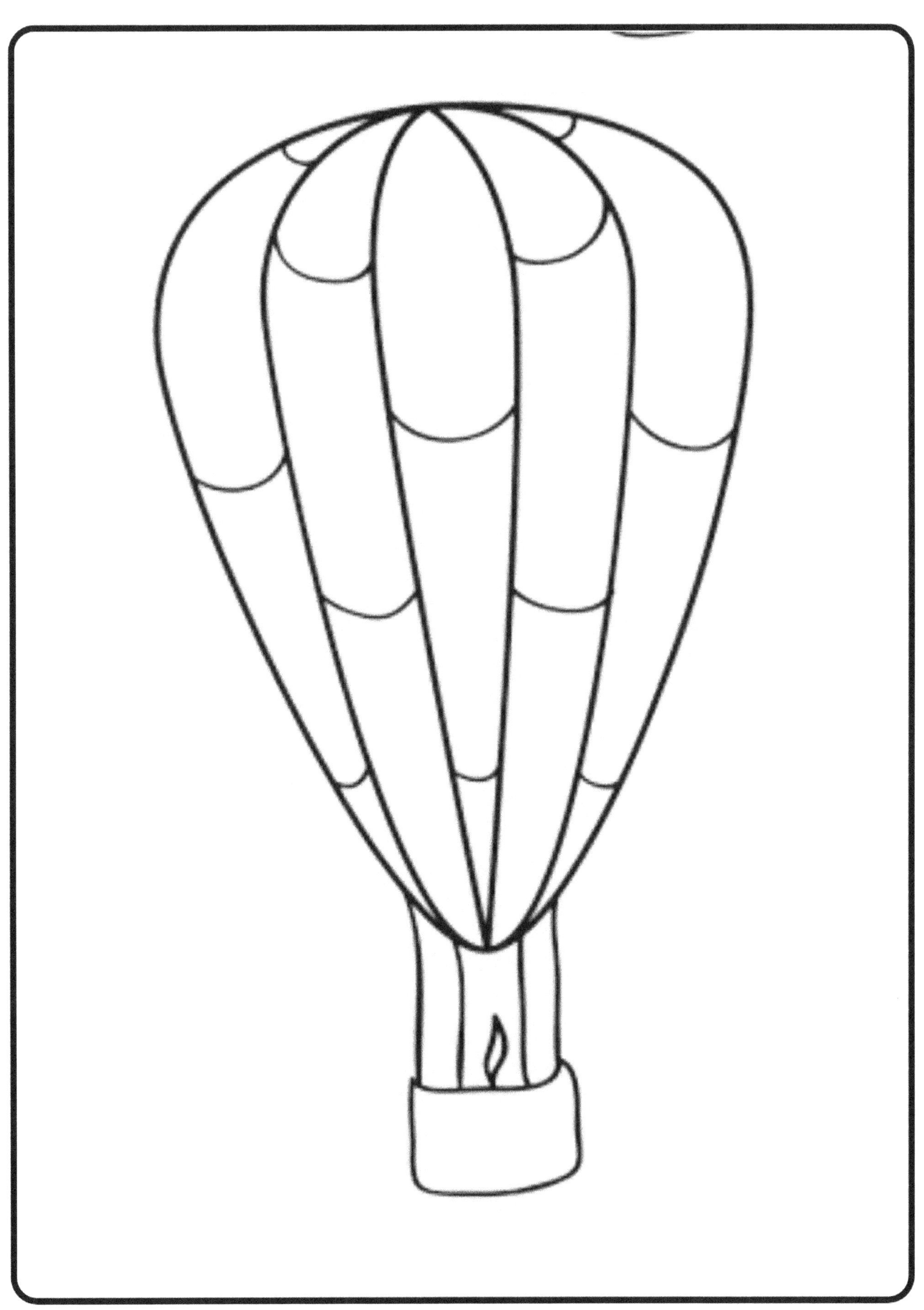

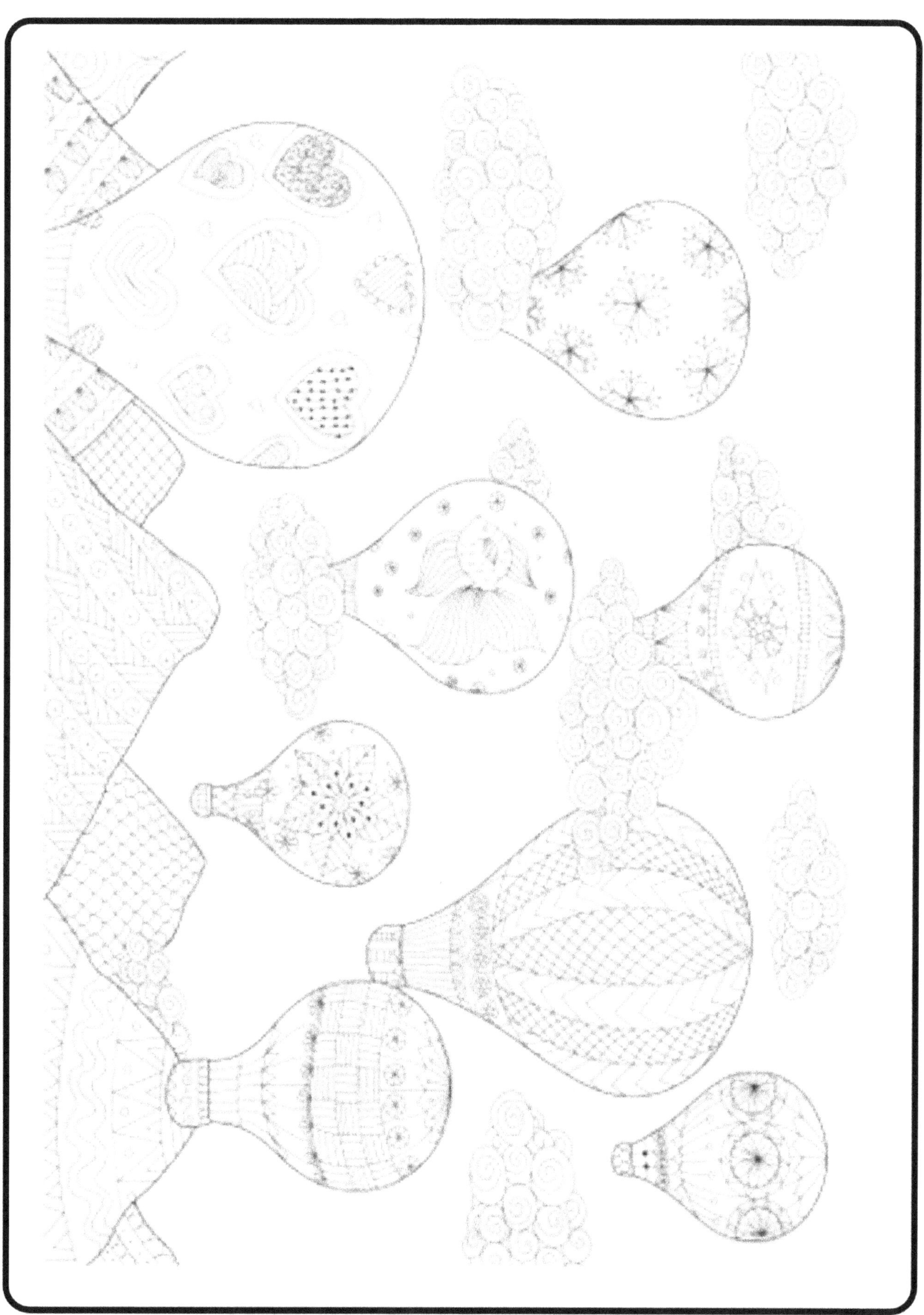

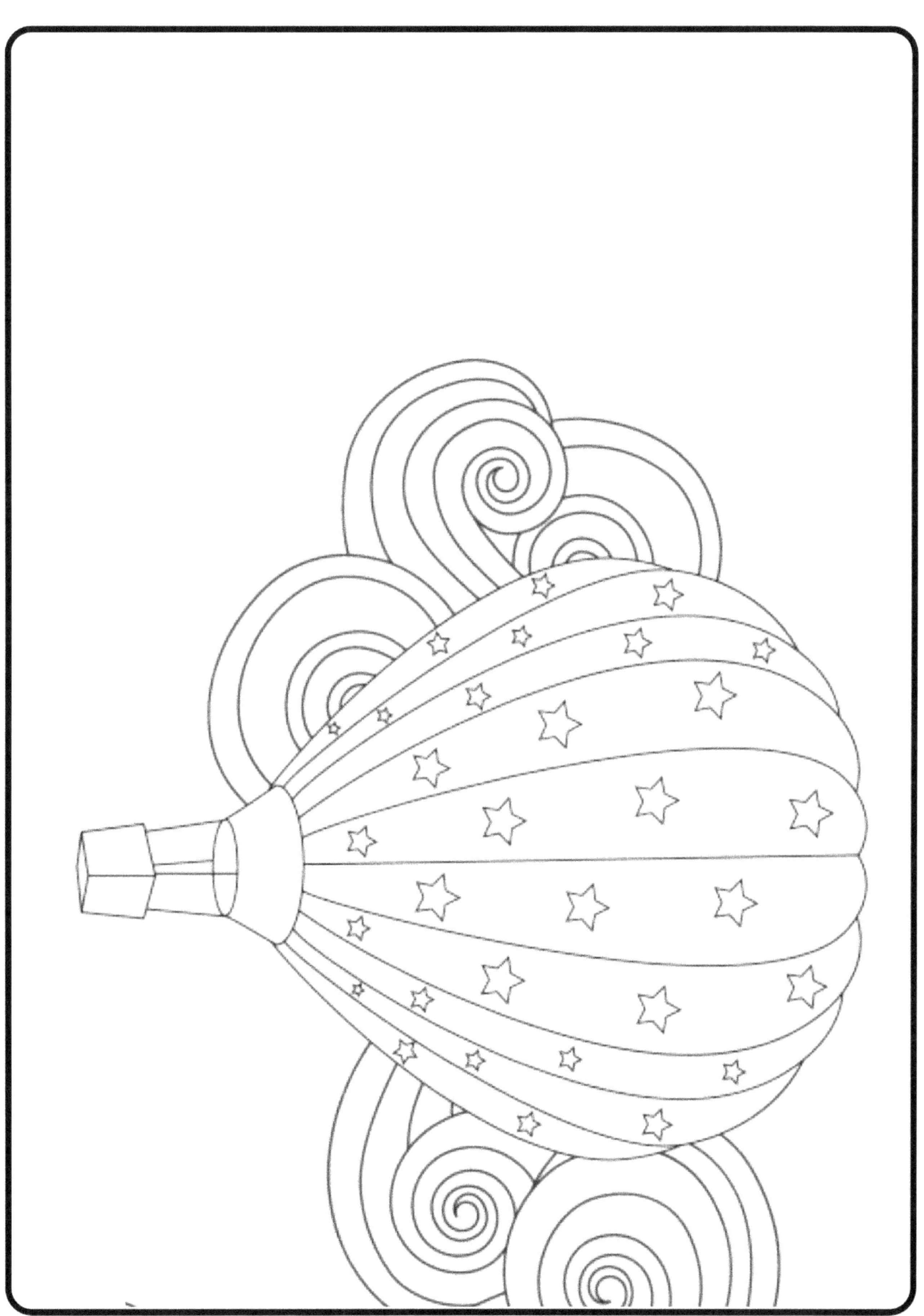

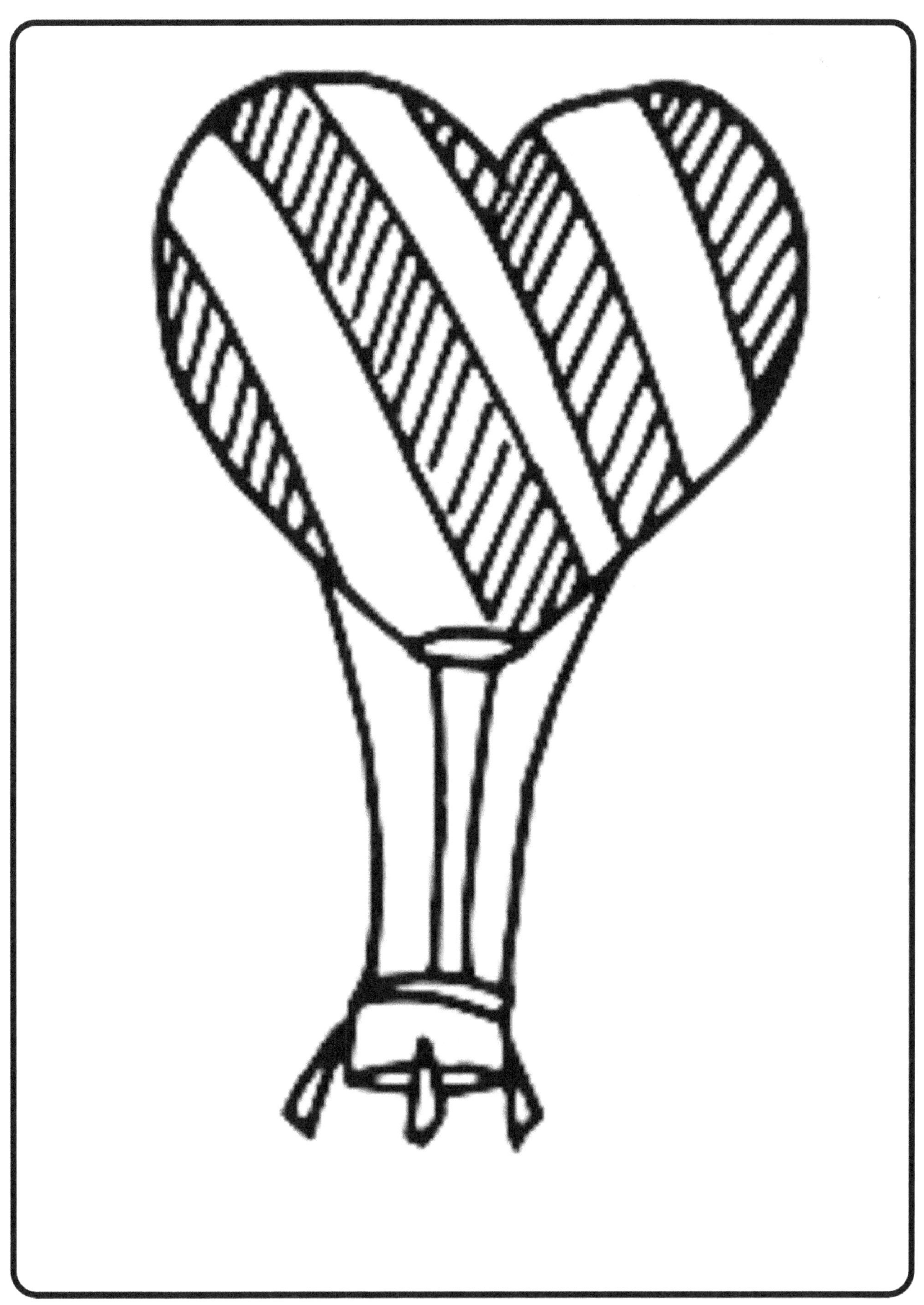